SIGHT

A TRUE BOOK®

by

Patricia J. Murphy

Children's Press®
A Division of Scholastic Inc.

New York Toronto London Auckland Sydney
Mexico City New Delhi Hong Kong
Danbury, Connecticut

A microscope can help you see very small things.

Reading Consultant
Nanci R. Vargus, Ed.D.
Assistant Professor
Literacy Education
University of Indianapolis
Indianapolis, IN

Content Consultant
Beth Cox
Science Learning Specialist
Horry County Schools
Conway, SC

Dedication:
To my mother and father

Library of Congress Cataloging-in-Publication Data

Murphy, Patricia J., 1963–
    Sight / by Patricia J. Murphy.
    p. cm — (A true book)
    Summary: Explores the sense of sight and the body parts used to pro-
duce it.
    Includes bibliographical references and index.
ISBN 0-516-22597-9 (lib. bdg.)   0-516-26968-2 (pbk.)
    1. Vision—Juvenile literature. 2. Eye—Juvenile literature. [1. Vision.
2. Eye. 3. Senses and sensation.] I. Title. II. Series.
QP475.7 .M87 2003
612.8'4
                                                    2001008341

Contents

You use your eyes all the time to learn more about the world around you.

See for Yourself

The sense of sight seems rather simple. When you want to see something, you look at it. Your eyes are constantly moving and taking pictures of the world around you. You don't even have to think about it!

Your eyes, however, must complete a long list of steps in

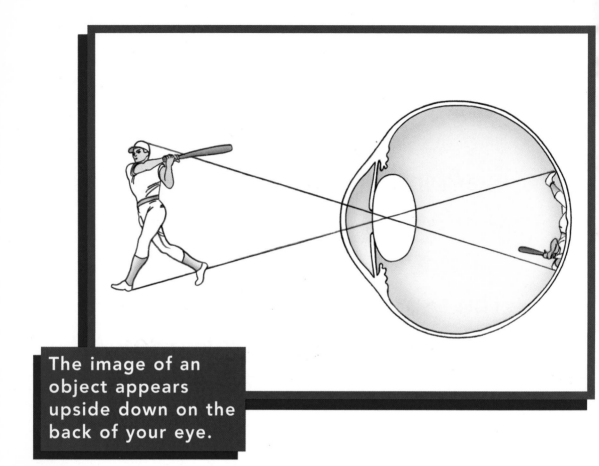

order for you to see. To begin
with, your eyes need light. It is
the light that comes from objects
that triggers your sense of sight.

When you watch a ball game, the light that bounces off the diamond, the ball, or a player enters your eye. Your eye then refracts, or bends, the light. The lens in your eye then focuses or centers these images on the back of your eye.

These images are turned into special messages, or **nerve impulses**. The messages travel through your eye to the brain through its optic nerve. The optic nerve leads to the brain.

It is the path your nerve impulses travel along.

Picture a batter hitting a home run. After he hits the ball, he must run the bases to home plate. Your eye's nerve impulses are like the player. The optic nerve is like the path he takes around the bases. Home plate is like the brain. Only when your brain receives the nerve impulses from the optic nerve is your eye able to see. Your eye hits a home run.

Like a batter hitting a home run, your nerve impulses take messages from your eyes all the way to your brain.

Your two eyes see very different views of the world. With your right eye, you see one view of a batter. You see another view of the batter

Your sight allows you to see things that are standing still or moving fast.

with your left eye. Your brain sorts out these images so that you see one view.

With sight, you can see the shape of the diamond and the color of the players' uniforms. You can see the movement of the ball and the stillness of the pitcher. Your eyes can see a fly ball coming near you or a ball going far away from you, out of the ballpark.

The Blind Spot

Each eye has a blind spot. It is located where the optic nerve leaves the eye and leads to the brain. This spot has no nerve impulses. As a result, no messages or impulses are sent to your brain. Your eye cannot see from the blind spot.

To check out your blind spot, close your right eye. Look at the dot on this page. Move the book toward your face. Do this until the *x* next to it disappears. The *x* appears on your blind spot so it is out of sight!

Your Eyes at Work

In order for your eyes to work, a chain of events must happen—and keep on happening. Each part of the eye has a special job and a certain time to do it.

To start your eye working, light must pass through your eye's **cornea**, or its thin, clear, protective layer. The light then

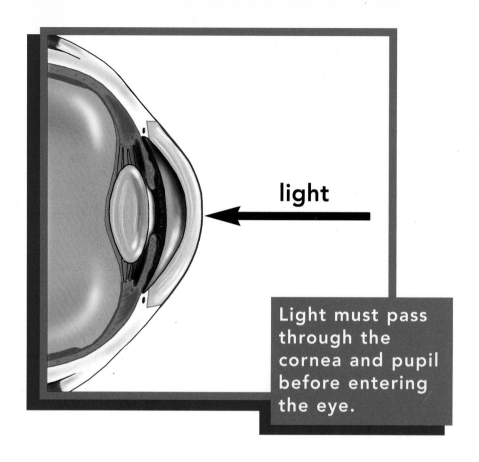

light

Light must pass through the cornea and pupil before entering the eye.

passes through the **pupil**. The pupil is the round, black opening in the center of your eye. The pupil opens and closes to let light in and out. The **iris** is the colored part of the eye. It is a muscle that controls the amount of light that enters the pupil.

In low light, the iris causes the pupil to expand or grow bigger. This increases the amount of light that enters the

A pupil will open wide in low light (left) and will become smaller in bright light (below).

pupil. In bright light, the iris contracts and makes the pupil smaller. This reduces the amount of light that enters the pupil. The iris protects your eye by keeping harmful, bright light from entering the pupil. Too much bright light can damage the eye's retina.

Upon entering the pupil, the light reaches the eye's lens. The lens is right behind pupil. It refracts, or bends, the light that comes into the pupil. The cornea helps with this bending, too. It then focuses an image on the back layer of the eye, or retina.

The retina has millions of light-sensitive nerve cells. These cells react to the light. They send nerve impulses or messages to the eye's optic nerve.

From the optic nerve, the impulses from both eyes go

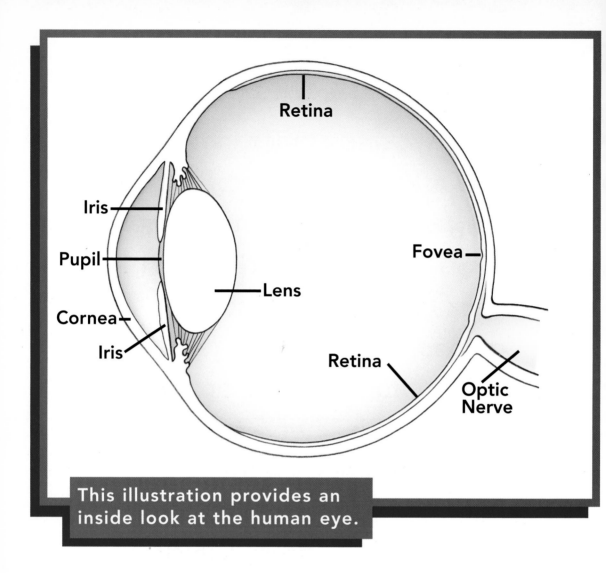

Retina

Iris—

Pupil—

Cornea—

Iris—

Lens

Fovea—

Retina

Optic
Nerve

This illustration provides an
inside look at the human eye.

to the brain. These impulses
cross through the base of the
brain, or optic chiasma. There,

the nerves sort out the right and left side of your eyes' images. The right-side images move to the right side of the **visual cortex**. The left-side images go to the left side.

The visual cortex is located in the back of the brain, or the occipital lobe. Its job is to make sense of what your eyes see. This is not an easy task. The images that appear on the retina are upside down and backwards.

It's Really the Retina

The retina's light-sensitive nerve cells react to light. These nerve cells have special names. They are called rods and cones. They allow you to see color and black and white.

Each eye has 125 million rods. The rods can be found all over the retina. They are called rods

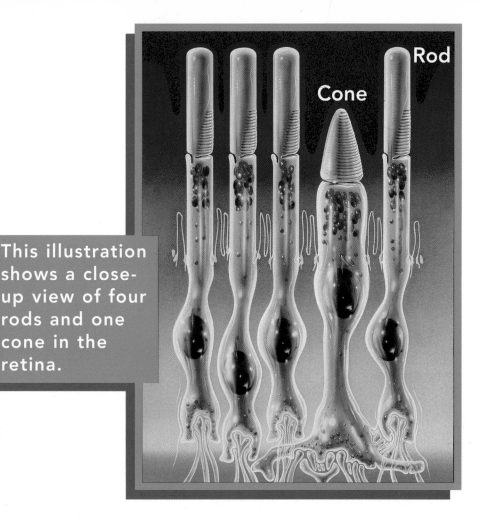

Cone

Rod

This illustration shows a close-up view of four rods and one cone in the retina.

because of their shape. Rods pick up black, white, and shades of gray. They help your eyes see in low light.

Each eye has 7 million cones. The cones are found in the center, or **fovea**, of the eye. They are named cones because of

Red cones help you see red light.

their shape. Cones pick up color and bright light all around you. There are three kinds of cones. They are red, blue, and green.

Red cones allow the eye to see red light. Blue cones react to violet-blue light. Green cones react to yellow-green light. When they work together, you can see all the colors.

When light hits the rods and cones, they send their color messages through their **nerve fibers** to the optic nerve. These

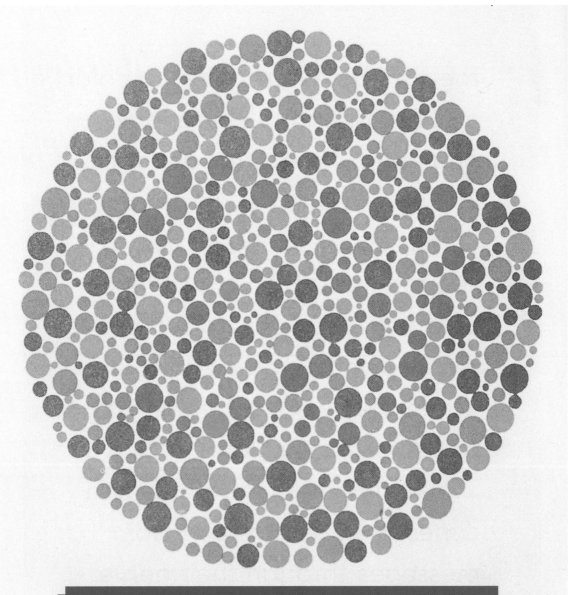

Can you see the number 29 in this picture?
If you can't, you might be color blind.

messages travel along the optic nerve to the brain. The brain then records the colored images and your eyes see color.

Some people cannot see colors the way most people do. They have color blindness. Many people with color blind-ness cannot see red and green. These colors appear gray. Other people may be unable to see pairs of different colors.

When Eyes Can't See

Some people see perfectly. Their eyes have perfect or 20/20 vision. They can see things clearly up to 20 feet (6 meters) away.

Other people have trouble seeing anything clearly. They may have been born with eye problems or have eye diseases. They may have injured their eyes.

With 20/20 vision, you can see objects far away.

Some people are born blind. Others become blind. People with limited vision or blindness

A young girl works with her teacher to read a book printed in Braille. Braille allows people who are blind to read using their sense of touch.

must use their other senses, such as hearing and touch, to see the world. Nearsightedness, farsightedness, and astigmatism are common vision problems.

People who are born near-sighted can see things close-up.

They cannot see things clearly that are faraway or at a distance though. This causes problems when they play catch or ride bicycles.

A person who is nearsighted could see this flower clearly, but the building in the background would appear blurry.

People are nearsighted because their eyes are too long from front to back. Their lenses or corneas may be too curved. The light that enters the eye focuses on a point in front of the retina. In a normal eye, the light that enters the eye focuses on the retina.

People who are born far-sighted can see things far away. However, they cannot see near or close-up. This is a problem when they read or use a computer.

A person who is farsighted could see the building in the distance clearly, but the flower would be blurry.

When people are farsighted, their eyes are too short from front to back. Their corneas may also be too flat. The light that enters the eye focuses on a point at the back of the retina. This causes close-up things to be blurry.

When people reach the age of forty, the lenses in their eyes become harder and less bendable. They do not curve or flatten to focus like they used to. This condition is called presbyopia. Presbyopia is a type of farsightedness. People with presbyopia cannot see things close-up.

People with astigmatism have lenses, corneas, or both

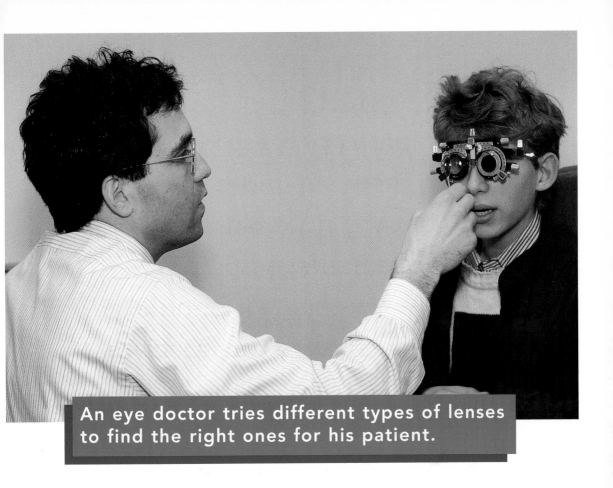

An eye doctor tries different types of lenses to find the right ones for his patient.

that are too flat. Things look wavy and twisted to them. People with astigmatism, nearsighted vision, or farsighted vision need special glasses.

The lenses of these glasses help them see more clearly. To get the right lenses, people must see an eye doctor.

Eye doctors test people's eyes. First, they put special drops in their patients' eyes. These drops make the pupil bigger. Then the doctor looks into the patient's eyes to see how they refract, or bend, light.

If there is a problem, eye doctors can prescribe or say what lenses should correct it.

An eye doctor checks to see how a patient's eyes are reflecting light.

They can prescribe glasses and contact lenses. Sometimes they perform surgery to correct vision problems.

The Ophthalmologist— The Eye Doctor

Ophthalmologists are doctors. They treat eye problems, injuries, and diseases. Many of these doctors perform surgery on eyes.

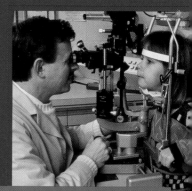

An ophthalmologist examines a patient's eyes.

To become an ophthalmologist, you should love—or at least like— school. Ophthalmologists must attend twelve years of school after high school! First, they must attend four years of college and another four years of medical school. Next, they must have one year of practice. Then, they must have three years of training! After they are done, they must pass a test and get a license to practice.

An optometrist helps a young girl pick out frames for her lenses.

Other people work with eyes. Optometrists are trained to prescribe glasses and contact lenses. Opticians make and fit glasses.

Take Care of Your Eyes

Your sight is the most important sense you have. Almost everything you do, you need your eyes. There are many things you can do to protect your sight:

• Keep sharp and pointed objects away from your eyes. They may cause injury or blindness.

• Don't rub your eyes if you get something in them. Instead, rinse them out with cool water. If you cannot do it yourself, get medical help.

• Wear glasses or goggles while playing sports. Many athletes wear them to avoid injury.

• Protect your eyes from bright lights. Do not look directly at the sun. These things can damage your eyes. Remember to wear sunglasses in the sunlight.

Los Angeles Dodgers pitcher Eric Gagne (left) wears glasses during a baseball game. Wearing sunglasses help protect your eyes (below).

Make sure you have enough light when working on your homework, and remember to take breaks to give your eyes a rest.

• Sit in well-lit areas when you read or do homework. If you don't, you could strain your eyes. Also, take breaks when reading or working on the computer.

• Eat foods like carrots and green and yellow fruits and vegetables. These foods are filled with vitamin A. Vitamin A helps keep your eyes healthy and seeing clearly.

Certain foods, such as carrots, are good for your eyes.

• Get plenty of rest. Sleep lets your eyes rest and renew.

• See an optometrist or an eye doctor if you have headaches or trouble seeing. Eye doctors can check your vision. They can prescribe glasses if you need them.

Don't take your sight for granted. You have only two eyes. If you take care of them, you will see for a lifetime.

Facts About Sight

- Your eyes are about the size of Ping-Pong balls.

- They measure almost 1 inch (2.5 cm) in diameter.

- Most people's eyes are 2.5 inches (6 cm) apart.

- Your eyes have six muscles that move them up, down, and all around.

- Your eyes' irises are as unique as you are. No two are alike!

- Your brow bones, eyebrows, eyelids, and eyelashes act like a cleaning and security system for your eyes!

To Find Out More

Here are some additional resources to help you learn more about the sense of sight:

Books

Ballard, Carol. **How Do Your Eyes See?** Raintree Steck-Vaughn, 1998.

Goldstein, Margaret J. **Eyeglasses.** Carolrhoda Books, Inc., 1997.

Green, Patrick. **Seeing is Believing**. Silver Burdett Press, 1996.

Hartley, Karen and Chris Marco. **Seeing in Living Things.** Heinemann, 2000.

Hurwitz, Sue. **Sight.** Rosen Publishing, 1997.

Pluckrose, Henry. **Seeing.** Gareth Stevens, 1995.

Pringle, Laurence. **Explore your Senses.** Benchmark Books, 2000.

Organizations and Online Sites

All About Vision
http://www.allaboutvision.com

This online site is full of information on eyes.

American Academy of Ophthalmology
http://www.aao.org

Find out more about the eye and the study of Ophthalmology.

The Hadley School of the Blind
700 Elm Street
Winnetka, IL 60093
http://www.hadley-school.org

This special school helps blind people live normal lives. Learn how they do it and about the school.

KidsHealth
http://www.kidshealth.org

Learn all sorts of healthy things about your eyes and your body!

Seeing, Hearing, and Smelling the World
http://www.hhmi.org/senses/

This site has lots of information on the brain and the senses. It also has a large glossary of terms on sight, hearing, and smelling.

Your Gross and Cool Body: The Sense of Sight
http://yucky.kids.discovery.com/noflash/body/index.html

Get answers to your questions about your eyes and more!

Important Words

cornea the tough, see-through outer layer of your eye, it covers the pupil and iris

fovea the center of your retina, it is where vision is the clearest

iris the colored part of your eye, it is a muscle that controls the amount of light that passes through your eye's pupil

nerve fiber a thin fiber or tube-like material where messages are sent between the brain and the spinal cord to let you see, feel, and move

nerve impulse an electrical reaction sent along a nerve to the brain

pupil the black, round opening in the center of your eye, it is where light enters your eye

visual cortex the back of the brain where images are received from the eye

Index

Meet the Author

Patricia J. Murphy writes children's storybooks, non-fiction books, early readers, and poetry. She also writes for magazines, corporations, educational publishing companies, and museums. She lives in Northbrook, Illinois.

Patricia has blue eyes. She likes to use them to look at paintings in art museums, watch baseball games, spy the stars in the sky, and see the faces of her family.